BOTANICALS

Ben Verinder

frosted fire

Frosted Fire Firsts Pamphlet Award 2021

© 2021 Ben Verinder

Ben Verinder has asserted his right under the Copyright, Design, and Patents Act to be identified as the author of this work.

All rights reserved. No part of this publication may be reproduced, stored in a retrieval system or transmitted in any form or by any means without the written consent of the author, nor otherwise circulated in any form of binding or cover other than that in which it is published and without a similar condition being imposed on a subsequent purchaser.

As a winner of Frosted Fire Firsts Award 2020, Ben Verinder has given permission for these poems to be published in this pamphlet by:

Frosted Fire
77 Tennyson Road, Cheltenham, GL51 7DD
01242 220860
wildfire-words.com

First Edition October 2021

ISBN 978-1-8384357-3-8

Designed and typeset in Times New Roman and Calibri by Frosted Fire

Cover art by Marilyn Timms, *layout by* Howard Timms

Printed and bound by Book Printing UK

Acknowledgements

I am grateful to the editors of the following publications in which some of these poems, or earlier versions of them, first appeared: *Brittle Star, Obsessed with Pipework, Carillion* and *The Blue Nib*. *Thyme* was longlisted for the 2020 National Poetry Competition.

Many thanks to John Stammers for his wisdom, enthusiasm and expertise, to the City Lit advanced poetry group for its continued support and Tim Ross for getting me started. A particular thank you to Sarah Gibbons for her generosity in responding to impromptu requests for feedback. Thank you to the tutors and mentors: Ella Frears, Seán Hewitt, Katharine Towers, Judy Brown, Katy Evans-Bush and John Glenday. A hearty thanks to Howard and Marilyn Timms for their encouragement and hard work in bringing this pamphlet to life. Thank you and much love to Kelly for her encouragement and patience.

Contents

Seed envelopes 9
Fern 10
White barley 11
Charms against the season 12
Bay 13
Vegetable patch as a meditative exercise 14
The figs are ripe 15
Peas 16
Rosemary, ground elder 17
Dandelion 18
Sloes 19
L'albero spezzato 20
giant poppy 21
Pears 22
Ratalang 23
Each day before a screen 24
The secret 25
Ash ....
Thyme ....

BOTANICALS

Seed envelopes

If I open them, next year happens.
Cherry, Tigerella, Santorini seeds
spooned into water jars –
gel sac sloughed like hours and surfaced as scum –
then strained, dried on a blank strip of card
and scraped into these manilla stops.
                                         Tonight
brings a balding thrush to the damson tree
and a warm breeze.
                          Those shortly to be born
don't comprehend the fact. Those soon to die
survive.
        I lock the envelopes in a pine chest
and turn off the potting shed lights.

Fern

'We have the receipt of fern seed, we walk invisible' (Henry IV, Part 1, Act IV, 4)

We stood naked before the French window
hand in hand and watched the badgers –
the smallest having trapped
his head in the food bin, clashed
it along the patio until we woke
then slopped it off like a sweaty helmet –
and wondered whether it was not moonlight
and thick glass that made us imperceptible
to them but the evening's walk through bracken
and we were the shepherd on the Isle of Arran
who crossed a ferny meadow to find his children
no longer saw him and could not decide
which was more thrilling: the glint of freedom
or trespass from one world into the next.

White barley

If you pour your voice deep into the cracks
along the footpaths down at Sterling Farm
it will be lost. The world is hotter
than it should be and the fields are mostly
moonlight and dust. Thistle tuft and
seed pods snap like spit on an anvil.
Even the barley has been thirsted
to a maltghost haunting the skillet barns.
When the rain finally arrives
it will fall like good money after bad.

Charms against the season

Inside the glasshouse
the smell of loam.
Jewelled flies whisk against hexagonal panes.

A child peels open
a pod between her thumbs
the way one might peer into a tiny book.

Along my forearm
the eleven-digit number
of a girl from Isfahan.

A robin carols
from the canopy of palms.
Women lean to touch an unfamiliar flower.

Plump and gradual carp
suck at the waterline. I carry their colours
in the rainbows of my steamed-up spectacles.

Bay

In the Great Plains Lightning Storms, one of the few settlements in South Dakota not to catch fire will be the city of Bay (pop 22,359), so called because every February twenty third its streetlights, from the Dr Kenneth Fleish Memorial Hall to the skate park – a former landfill site – are garlanded with wreaths of bergamoty bay. When the camera crews arrive, Mayor Taylor will show them the crisped circles smelling of linalool and cineole, of cold creams and ski chalets, stand on a crate of Gasper's oranges and say: "You betcha, the lighting came pert near to these stores but hit instead every wreath along Main Street and tuckered out. Round here we're kinda hushed. Slow with strangers. I figure we're not an easy place to set alight."

Vegetable patch as a meditative exercise

Take a deep breath.
Each leaf is a modification of consciousness.

What do you want from this ground?
See if you can relinquish that.

Consider the sounds in the garden:
how they arrive, depart
and you are helpless to resist.

The moment you know you are lost
come back to the radishes, the beans.
You too are a matter of experience.

When you observe a cabbage white is present
see if you can accept the insect
as a change in your relationship with the brassicas.

Be aware of the sensation
of standing beside the rhubarb.
Let your mind be the space in which clouds appear.

The figs are ripe

and I am back in Cyprus
as we breakfast in the marble light
a salty linseed-blue day stretching over the village
its smell of thyme and ruminants
the fishing boats the quiet sea

cradling the first extraordinary fruit
of my parent's Nottinghamshire garden
dew burnt off the yellow lawn
summer burst open and already ruining
school bags packed in the hall

back among this cottage's bowls and baskets
figs hoarded in the stopped clocks of jars
the baking paper tarred in their collapse
skins smeared and furred in the compost bowl
beyond the common cauterising wasps the careless rain

Peas

I abandon my plans to establish
this afternoon the bounds of the settlement

since they constrict. My new home shrinks.
I squeeze outside to watch the sky fall;

clouds compact to mist, grind down to dew
horizons advance from every side.

A field corrugates – sprouting peas.
Fir copse falls into itself like praying hands.

Magpies rattle right beside the ear
and the end of the lane is in touching distance

postbox a retinal flare.
Kettled breezes press against me.

The sun – Makita worm-drive circular saw
biting into the treeline – splatters us with dusk

then buries itself in the ridge.
Darkness is immediate as the back of the eyes.

Rosemary, ground elder

I crawled under this rosemary bush
to dig ground elder out of the bed
but its dismal yellow hands cling
to the shrub's roots, snap
at the knuckle. A buried tip
is enough to poke it back
out of the soil. So rosemary persists;
this plant survived you by twenty years
as does the wish that you had time
to explain how much of life
is digging and how grief
wound tight round memory
cannot be weeded out but flowers
as snow-in-the-mountain.

Dandelion

Wet the bed, butter flower, worm rose
lover's test, palace guard, wish mill, pig's nose
we want this small plant to be so much
bald patch, seed clock, treasure chest, milk witch
when we could be satisfied with it as salad
wine, rubber, beer, dye, fodder, instead
of filling its head with ideas, each
attached to a parachute of speech
and nothing in field or forest reminds me
so much of you, the 'what do you want to be?'
I ask repeatedly when I should be content
with sunshine, medal of excellence
little flower, lion's teeth, eight year old
dandelion daughter, meaning gold.

Sloes

I have convinced you it is the sip of ruby-coloured gin
that warms my blood on colder nights
so here we are among the hedgerow's late summer glut
your little hand tenderly picking berries into the tub
feeling for a pulse through their powder-blue skins.

L'albero spezzato

This beech played its notes of leaves;
they fell through autumn's bars
tenderly like settling light.

Storms are too restless to learn
and last night
one picked up the tree and broke it.

So many splintered instruments!
I wonder whether, when you are older,
there will be music here.

giant poppy

for most of the year
the main sequence of growth
or black dwarf of seed
except the two weeks in summer
when they supernova
amassing our admiration
and planetary bees

Pears

I hold your oedematous hand   beneath the pot-bellied fruit
as my other ripens a nipple   even the sky is overdue
your kiss smells of raspberry and pineapple
wasps scalpel grass   while we undress
to the breathing exercise
plums   apples   blackberries
pears

Ratalang

our eucalyptus love
it was mulberries and wild figs
bone fruit   red saltbush   sweet blue appleberry

it was leaf wattle   yellow thyme   rice flowers

our love was the headland
the true names of the headland

shrunk now to salt winds and blusters
forgotten dreaming
a pile of broken pipi shells

Each day before a screen

Cornflowers are the earth dreaming of sky
but we make the fields work so hard for us
there are no flowers here

and it is too long since
I let a thought grow raggedly and wild
the colour of a summer evening.

The secret

We like to keep it among friends
be sure you're here for good
before we say the name and mark it on a map.
Some people, naturally, never learn.

You'll understand if and when we let you know
the way the beech trees meet the bluebells
in the crucible of wood
pure lime and indigo.

First time I saw it I was straight back in chemistry
last lesson Easter term
and tricks they only showed to those who'd stuck around –
that one with acid, blotting paper, sweets.

Thyme

Thyme flowers hold the souls of murdered English
but I forget and pluck a sprig
which is why the gamekeeper Puddephat's Inverness coat
and smashed-in-head appear on the patio.
"This is awkward," I say, "your great-great-granddaughter
lives next door and if she sees you…"
"She won't," he splutters. "I last only as long as this oil and lemon scent."
Which is enough for him to describe how much he wished
if he had the time again
he had taken a gun up to the Nowers that stormy night
instead of an elder stick
and how long he had lain before puttering out
and which of the poachers did for his friend Crawley
and which for him
his jaw like a gate unlatched by the wind
socket a charcoal pit
and how the skulled and the hanged and the black-throated women
lament their children by ringing these pale pink bells.

Ash

Like plague doors, I remember Margaret said
each tree along the ridge splodged with paint. They felled them all;
sawdust scratching your eyes when you went out with the dog.
Every block of Kerry Gold in the shop sprouted mould
but none of us took it for a sign
and Barbara said it was just the blinking fridge.
Then sweet itch among the horses in the Mason's field;
the bay mare bit a chunk out of her own backside.
Adders, a nest, in scrub between the tennis court and the Pyke's.
Jenny Scattergood found them, called the RSPCA
said she bloody well knew the difference
between a viper and a slow worm thank you
but by the time the man arrived they had slithered off.
Five kids on Summer Hill came out in warts.
On their faces! Can you imagine?
It was only then that Margaret cottoned on.
They had already started cutting into Sprockett's Wood
and that, of course, is when the real trouble starts.